Release Your Grief

WENDY MIDDLEHURST

DEDICATION

This book is dedicated to all the little girls who grew up without a dad.

To the little girls who wondered why they weren't enough.

Who struggled to let genuine love in, and instead just seemed to attract more men who hurt them.

To those little girls whose heart hung on to a tiny piece of hope for a fairy-tale 'happily ever after' right up until the end, even though logic had told them for years not to be so stupid.

To the little girls who are now grown up. Who are now the guardians of their own still hurting inner child.

To you, I'm with you. I hear you. I'm doing it too, and its shit.
We never asked for this. We never asked for these dads, but we can get through this – together.

CONTENTS

Acknowledgments

Poem

ACKNOWLEDGMENTS

To my family, thank you for putting up with the mood swings!

I hope no-one in my immediate family reads this book and feels any kind of upset. This is *my* story only, and I know we all experience things in a very different way. I also know that we all only do what we think is best, with the skills, strength and knowledge that we have at the time.

To my colleagues who I consider my friends, thank you for also putting up with my mood swings and my epic rants!

To Cassandra Farren, thank you for your amazing group, your support and your encouragement – I would not have had the courage to do this without you.

To Michelle Emmerson thank you for your amazing Motherbooker program and for answering my endless questions. You seriously need a medal!

And to me, well done girl, you've come a bloody long way!

RELEASE YOUR GRIEF

TO MY DAD WHO LEFT ME

I cannot stand by your grave and weep.
You were never there, you did not keep
the promises a parent should make to
their child.
To love,
protect,
support,
and guide.

I will not stand at your grave and weep.
Because you let me cry myself to sleep.
Night after night,
On my own
No explanations
No word – you'd gone.

I won't let myself stand at your grave and weep.
I'm protecting the child that you did not keep
safe from the pain of rejection at eight.
She's still inside me and her heart still breaks,
to know that her father just didn't care.
To know that he chose to not be there
at every important event in her life;
he missed it all
to live his own life.

So I will never stand at your grave and cry
You let me down,
and never told me why.

………yet, here I stand at your grave…………. and I weep.

Wendy Middlehurst (21/09/2018)

INTRODUCTION

When my absent father (or twat as he's more commonly known) died I was actually a bit lucky.

You see I happen to be a bereavement counsellor working with a beautiful bunch of counsellors who let me rant and rave. They let me cry, let me call the bastard every name under the sun; they realised just how complicated and shit the whole thing was and never told me to shut up. They never told me to be, or to feel, anything other than what I was feeling. I was very present in my own grief and could recognise what was happening.

It didn't stop anything hurting though. It didn't make anything better in that respect, but it stopped me thinking I was going mad and heading for the local mental hospital!

I know that most people don't have those luxuries that I had. Don't have that awareness of grief. And aren't surrounded by a bunch of beautiful counsellors.

So, I wanted to write this book for you, so you have someone who's been through something similar. So, you have somewhere to turn for peace of mind. To know you're not crazy. To know that there is actually no correct way to feel or grieve when an absent parent dies, and to know you're not alone.

Your story won't be exactly the same as mine. It can't be. No two people have exactly the same story. Even twins experience things slightly differently. And grief, wow...grief is so unique that even you won't experience it the same way twice. It shows up differently every time. That's one of the reasons it's so fucking hard to deal with, and one of the reasons why when your well-meaning friends/families/co-workers say, 'I understand what you're going through' you want to punch them square in the face! Because they don't get it, they don't understand, just like I won't

1

completely get it. But I hope I get close. I hope some of this resonates with you. I hope that parts of this book help you to feel 'normal' (whatever the hell that is anyway) and validated. I hope this book helps in some small way because us kids whose dads couldn't be arsed will have some similarities, we will share some common thoughts/feelings and struggles. Especially when the selfish bastards decide to die. That's when it goes from properly shite to shite of epic, confusing proportions! These absent fathers have a hell of a lot to answer for that's for sure!

I don't know at what point in your journey this book will land in your hand, but I'm a big believer in everything happening for a reason and I trust that the universe will bring it to you at the correct time.

Grief due to a bereavement never ends.

Never.

There is no getting over it. No end of the process. No reaching the finish line. It stays with us for as long as we're alive.

It never ends, but it *changes*. It *shifts*, it *moves*. It affects us in different ways at different times. It becomes more familiar to us, and we learn to adapt to it. We carry it differently that's all, but it never goes away. It can't because that person is never coming back. They will never give us the answers we seek, and there is no time machine that can take us back and give us the parent we should've had in the first place.

We will carry this complicated grief forever but that doesn't scare me, and I don't want it to scare or depress you either. It's a part of us, yes. It's our story, yes. But the control now is ours. We can learn from it and heal, or we can get bitter and twisted and stuck. Please don't choose the latter.

Let it teach you just how strong you are to have grown up with the chain around your neck of early rejection.

Let it teach you more about yourself.

Allow your emotions to show you the parts that need healing and give them attention. Be the beautiful, nurturing parent to your hurt inner child and soothe it, reassure it, tell it that it was never their fault. That they are worthy of love, that they are loveable. That *you* will never reject them. That you will allow it to cry and to shout and to misbehave, and you will love it anyway. You will hold it and heal it and love it.

You hold the keys to your own healing, and to releasing your grief.

KNOWING IT WAS ALWAYS COMING

Let's face it, we've all thought about it. How will I feel when he's actually dead? Will I be bothered? Will it screw me up even further?

I'd just been talking about it to a friend about a fortnight before he died. I must've been frigging psychic!

I'd been preparing for this day for twenty-eight years. Wondering what it would be like when he wasn't just AWOL anymore, he was actually dead and gone.

Wondering how it would feel.

Would I go to the funeral?

Would I even know that he'd died?

Would anyone bother to tell me?

Would I care?

Would I go the funeral simply out of curiosity?

Would I be welcome?

Would it give me any answers?

Would it just give me more questions?

I bet we all think about it. All of us rejected, ditched daughters of dickhead dads. We all use our precious thinking time on this. And the sad truth is that we just haven't a clue. We've always been just guessing. Maybe some of us will think and feel and act in the way that they always thought they would. But I know some of us, just like me, won't. Their emotions will do something different and confusing.

The even sadder thing coming to mind as I write this, is just how many people there must be out there. Who are wondering whether they'll be bothered when their absent father does die?

Why does this happen so often? Why are there so many daughters like us? Why does this even have to be a thing? Why do these dads just leave? In an ideal world every daughter would be devastated when her dad dies

3

because he loved her, and she loved him. But we're not in the ideal world, we're in the real one. In the real-world dads leave. Our dads left. And it's shit.

THE SADNESS, THE PAIN, THE CRYING; THE LAST LITTLE CRUEL PIECE OF HOPE

The sadness was by far the hardest part of this whole shitty picture to deal with. It was the sadness that took me by surprise more than anything. Anger I expected. Arguments with family I half expected, but sadness....no, I wasn't prepared for that one. I wasn't prepared for the amount of crying either.

Crying. Crying. Crying.

Endless crying.

Heavy, ugly, painful sobs.

I just wanted to cry.

All the time.

I wasn't even sure what I wanted to cry about.

I just didn't expect that much crying.

This wasn't how it was meant to be! I wasn't supposed to be bothered! He didn't bother with me did he?!

Would he have even cried if I'd died?

He wouldn't even have known if I'd died!!

Emotions are shit sometimes. This wasn't how I thought it would be.

Tears, can you just fuck off please?!

It was so confusing to start with. I wasn't crying for him...how could I be? I didn't know him. I wasn't missing him....how could I be? There was nothing to miss.

I could only guess that I was crying for what would never be. For what I never had. For the very end, the very final end of hope.

5

But the cruellest twist is that I'm still hoping. Hoping that I'll get some closure from a medium, or in a dream or he'll speak or appear. I'm still searching and hoping. It's sad. It feels quite pathetic that still I haven't given up.

And I keep hoping that maybe there's some little pot of gold. An account he started for me years ago that's grown and grown and shows he did care after all. Or maybe there's a letter, or a trinket, or something he left for me. Something that shows that maybe, just maybe, I was on his mind and he did love me after all.

I feel sorry for myself. For that pathetic, hopeful child that still, after twenty-eight years can't accept completely that he just didn't fucking give a shit.

Come on Wendy, you need to accept it. You need to stop being eight and be thirty-six. Adult for fuck sake. You need to parent yourself, because no one is coming to save you – to rescue you. He never came when he was alive. He's certainly not going to do anything now he's dead. It's horrible, it is, but it's not going to change.

But, how the hell do I heal myself from this?
How do I soothe the hurting child within?
How do I rescue myself?
How do I heal this wound?

I just so desperately want to rest, to cry, to scream, to hurt. But I have to be a mam. I have to be a partner. I have to be a counsellor. I have to pay the bills.

Oh, what I would give to have time and space to heal.

The sadness hit me at the strangest of times, and in the strangest ways. The worst was in the first couple of weeks after he died – before the funeral in fact – I kept thinking that I'd seen him. Not in a weird ghostly kind of way, but in the way that I thought I'd seen him in the street, or at the shops or in the middle of Tesco. I'd see an old, grey haired, thin, tall man with glasses and my heart would leap. I'd think 'shit, there's my dad!' but then I'd realise that of course it wasn't... It couldn't possibly be. There will never be any random, chance meetings. I'll never ever just bump into him. I'll never wonder on my birthday or Christmas if this year a card will come......he's gone now. Totally and completely gone. Forever.

I hadn't actually realised I'd been doing that for twenty-eight years either. Subconsciously scanning every high street, every shop, every bar, every town, every motorbike, every restaurant, everything – everywhere, for twenty-eight long years. I hadn't realised that I had always been searching for him. And always wanting him to appear. Always wanting that one last chance reunion where he would see the error of his ways and be the dad I'd always wanted. I could be a father's daughter at last. One of those where they mean the world to their dad, and he's their 'rock and protector'. I always wanted that…always…and I should've had it. Its cruel that I didn't, and that I had to scan the aisles of Tesco hoping to magically find it one day.

It makes me feel so desperately sad that that was my life for so long. It feels like a great big bowling ball is inside my stomach, weighing me down. It feels awful. It feels so heavy. It feels so tragically final that I will never ever get to have what I spent so long hoping and searching for.

The sadness is for the end of hope.

When all hope goes, there's only sadness left. And for me, a very weird, empty acceptance that this is just the way it will always be.

THE WIZARD IS DEAD

The news is going to come in totally different ways for us all. You might get a phone call, you might get told in person, you might see it on social media. You might find out at the time of death or years after. We just never know how it's going to happen.

This is how it went for me...

The phone call came late at night – it woke me up. A phone call late at night is never going to be good news so answering it was a bit like sticking my head into a pan of boiling water – I just didn't want to do that. But, I did.

It was my sister.

Alison - "the wizard is dead"

(the 'wizard' was the codename my sister came up with so we could talk about him without nosey children knowing what we were on about basically. She coined the term based on the fact that his head was "full of magic" – or full of shit as I would say)

Me – "fuck off, no way! (silence)............shit!..........How do we tell Scarlet (our sixteen year old half-sister who grew up with him actually around) ....fuck, fuck, fuck, fuck..... aw fuck!"

She then proceeded to tell me the how and where and all that bit.

The conversation was a shock, of course it was, but it didn't really surprise me either. He was only sixty-five, but he'd been on borrowed time for years. Cancer diagnosed sixteen years ago, heavy smoker, even heavier drinker. Didn't look after himself. He was sixty-five years old but looked like a ninety-year-old smackhead.

What came next surprised me though.

Tears.......... real, heavy, sobbing tears. Painful ones.

Nearly three weeks later as I write this, they haven't stopped.

I wasn't ready for this pain. This was a lot of buried pain hitting some fresh new pain and it was combining to make a big old fucking painful mess.

This was my first indication that my emotions were just not going to do what I'd always thought they would.

GROWING UP AS A REJECTED CHILD – THE LASTING IMPACT

When you're only little and your dad leaves, you're forced to get to know painful and confusing emotions. I certainly grew up feeling confused, and feeling like;

"I'm not good enough"

"I'm not worth anything"

"I'm not loveable".

I constantly felt left out. I would constantly compare myself to the other children around me. I would constantly feel jealous. I became a very bitter, angry and unhappy child. I didn't like being different, I just wanted to be like everyone else, but I knew I couldn't be. I had no dad – they all did. Like it or not, I was different.

For some readers this part may not be the same as it was for me. Separated parents, single parents, gay parents, adopted parents; they're all very common now, but I was eight in 1990 and back then, where I lived, on a nice little private estate in the North East of England it wasn't common to have separated parents. I remember there was one lad being brought up by his grandparents I think, but everyone else, to my knowledge, had both parents. I must've stood out like a sore thumb. I felt like I did anyway. So, I quickly learned to be mean to other people to take the attention off me. And I was mean. I was a right nasty cow at times. That makes me sad now, because I know I was being a little bitch from a place of pain, but I didn't join those dots back then, why would I? I was only a little kid.

Jealousy and comparison became very familiar to me. I seemed to spend the whole of my teens comparing myself to other girls. They were always skinnier, prettier, nicer, happier, more talented, cleverer, more likely to do something with their lives, had nicer clothes, better hair – everything, just everything. Maybe other girls who have dad's do this too, but for me, I'd started to feel like I wasn't good enough when I was eight, so it just kept going. It was pretty exhausting to be honest. Feeling shit about yourself all the time is hard work.

Childhood as I remember it

I woke up on the first of December thinking about Christmas. My mind wandered from what time should we put our decorations up today, to what Christmases were like when I was a kid, and then before I knew it my mind was clawing at the past desperately trying to remember what life was like before my dad left.

Before my dad left, Christmases were good. The worst thing I remember about Christmas was complaining to my mam that I hadn't got a Pound Puppy and feeling annoyed, hard done to and upset. I think my mam had told me to stop being so ungrateful and such a little brat – fair enough comment I suppose. However, my grandparents turned up as they always did on Christmas Day and they'd got me one. I was so happy. My Christmas was perfect. I had nothing else to complain about. In fact, my whole childhood up to being eight years old, I had nothing to complain about. I don't remember any arguments, I don't remember feeling like I missed out on anything. I went to kids' parties, we had parties at our house. People were always visiting. I went outside and played. We had holidays. We had a car. We had a nice house. I went to a nice school. I don't remember feeling any different to anyone else at all. Life consisted of climbing trees, playing with Sylvanian families, playing out generally with the tribe of kids in the street, going and visiting my aunty Jean where we roamed around in wellies, stepping over cattle grids being careful not to fall in and break our legs, picking apples in the orchard and feeling so cosy in her little cottage with the real fire. Life for me anyway was idyllic. It was a childhood full of people, play, parties, presents, and fun. I was just me, happy little eight year old me, nothing to complain about, except not getting a Pound Puppy – which I got half an hour later.

Then it all changed.

It all changed with my sister on the way to school very bluntly and quite nastily saying, 'dad isn't coming back – he's gone'.

And that was it, he was gone. Trips to aunty Jeans were gone (she was my dad's sister), people stopped visiting, and it all changed. It changed in an instant. It changed without any explanation. Overnight I became very different. I became the kid in the class with no dad. The kid on free school meals. The kid who now had to make up stories about what she did at the weekend because writing 'my grandparents came to see us' every single weekend just didn't seem good enough. I wanted to write what the other kids wrote – I went swimming with my mam and dad, I went to a party, I had horse riding lessons, we went shopping.

I wanted to be just like everyone else, but I wasn't… Not anymore. I was the odd one out. And I've felt that way ever since.

The love void

The other thing that got me was always wanting to fill that void. The love and affection void. I remember always being so desperate to have a boyfriend. And I was never particularly selective – anyone who showed the slightest interest would do, I wasn't choosy at all. Which of course led to some absolute disaster choices.

Broken hearts do not choose wisely at all!

I went from disaster to disaster, with a slight detour to a total rescuer who actually started to show me what proper love looks like, to an enormous disaster followed by a few more disasters until I had finally flipped and was exploring this in personally therapy. I remember discussing the anger that I was feeling at being dumped yet again by another waste of space that I'd collected from an online dating site. There was a song around at the time and it was killing me every time I heard it;

Wildest dreams - Taylor Swift

I can't even explain what that song was doing to me at the time. It seemed to be on every single time I got in my car and put the radio on, and it was actually hurting me to listen to it. But weirdly, I loved it at the same time and would sing it with such force and passion that I just knew it was telling me something. I thought at the time it was linked to this bloke that had dumped me. I thought it was a broken heart kind of thing over him, but as I discussed it in therapy it just didn't make sense. I was livid with him for dumping me even though we'd known each other probably only a month and been on maybe four dates. He wasn't even that nice, or a particularly great catch, but again he was better than nothing to help me fill the lonely void. In my head, having a boyfriend/partner/husband meant I was actually lovable. So, I absolutely *had* to have one. The quality of the man was totally irrelevant.

So, we pulled this anger apart in therapy and at some point, I told my counsellor about this song that was constantly in my head and just wouldn't stop.

She was listened to me rant on and on, and tried to help me work it out. It was all very confusing for a bit but then she did two fantastic things that changed my life from that moment on......actually she did three.

First, she said to me something along the lines of,

"Yes, it's like you're throwing everything you've got at these men that have dumped you – like you're saying YOU WON'T FORGET ME YOU BASTARD!!"

Ping! Lightbulb starting to go off there...

Then she said,

"Just feel all that anger for a moment, don't try and move it - just feel it – feel as angry as you can. (I did, and it wasn't particularly pleasant)

"Keep feeling it, all that hate and anger. Now, who deserves this anger? Who would you actually like to throw it at?"

Boom!!

Big old, enormous penny dropped.

MY DAD!!

I want to throw it all at my dad!! I want to go around his house, bang on the door (I'd done this to the internet guy who'd dumped me – cringe!) I want to tell my dad what I think about *him*, send *him* angry, ranty, text messages. It was him I wanted to scream at and say, "How dare you leave me you bastard! How dare you forget me!! How dare you dump me!! Arsehole!!!! Fucking arsehole!!!"

That link, I'm sure had been obvious to everyone else for decades. Me choosing shit men, then acting like a woman possessed when I got dumped, then looking straight away for another one – anything will do – just so I'm not on my own and therefore lovable. It was all glaringly obvious to other people I'm sure, but to me the pennies hadn't dropped. It wasn't making sense in my head. But it did that day.

And what a relief that was!

The second thing my therapist did was discuss all kinds of different ways I could purge this anger out of me a bit more. We discussed burning things, writing things, chucking stones into rivers, dartboards with photos on – all sorts of safe ways of purging this anger that wouldn't land me in prison.

Just discussing how I could potentially do these things, actually purged a lot of the anger anyway.

I felt lighter, and so much calmer.

But then, the third thing was she also gave me a poem to read. The poem was;

She Let Go – Rev. Safire Rose

(I'd love to include the whole poem here, but for copyright reasons I can't. I urge you to look it up though, it's wonderful.)

And that was it. That was the third piece of the puzzle.

Later that day, at home on my couch, reading that poem, in the space of letting go, I let it all be. It was like a weight lifted, something inside me shifted and I knew that that cycle of anger would never happen again. No matter how many times I was dumped from that moment on, I knew I was never going to throw all the pain and anger that my dad deserved at them. What a relief it was to be free of that burden.

And, as luck would have it, two months later I went on one last internet date and met the love of my life, who as yet hasn't dumped me and I have no plans to dump him. It's amazing what shifts happen when you step out of old, unhelpful cycles.

Always longing for a 'normal' family

This one tripped me up constantly and caused me no end of heartache. Not only was I always desperate for love, I remember from a very young age being desperate to have children. I remember a teacher at school asking the class, "who wants to have children by the time they're twenty?" (haven't a clue why he was asking this – bit of a weird question now I think about it) and there was only me that put my hand up. But I meant it, I genuinely wanted children. I wanted a 'normal' family – a mam, a dad and a couple of sprogs. I thought it would be perfect. I could give them the life I hadn't had. I could give them 'a proper family'.

There's nothing wrong with that in itself, it's a perfectly nice thing to want. My problem lay in the fact that I had absolutely no real self-esteem, very little self-respect and I was happy to have any bloke that took an interest. So, my choice of father for my children was not the best one in the world, and I certainly didn't get the picture-perfect happy family I was looking for. I stayed in a very toxic and unhappy relationship for far longer than was good for my sanity, because I wanted to save my children from the pain of a broken home.

All I actually did was prolong my suffering and eventually there was no option but to separate.

The guilt I felt was enormous. For me, history, despite all my good intentions, had repeated itself. I was now the not so proud owner of a failed marriage and 3 children from a broken home. There comes a point though, when you *have* to do what needs to be done for your own sanity and protect yourself. I still feel bad that I chose badly, but I can't dwell on that, I was just doing the best I could with what I knew at the time. If only I knew back then what I knew now, but hey ho, I'm sure everything happens for a reason. I've learned to change my response to not so great experiences from 'what was I thinking?' to 'what was I learning' and it helps, it really does.

His new family

This one was a mother fucker of kicks in the teeth. This one stung like a bitch. This one brought up all the smouldering feelings of not being good enough, not being likeable enough, or loveable enough, always being unwanted and second best and just poured petrol on the fire.

Seeing him be capable of being a dad to someone else was shit. I had let my brain grasp hold of the story that he was just a fucking waste of space with a million issues and was incapable of being a 'family man'. That story was easier to carry because it made it his fault instead of mine and that was much nicer. But when he became a dad to another child and actually bothered with that child and brought her up, that was a monumental kick in the teeth because it became (at least in my head) my fault again. Clearly, he *could* be a dad, he was doing it now. He had the ability. But he wasn't a dad to me, so that *must* be my fault. I clearly wasn't a nice enough, funny enough, lovely enough kid to want to be around. That's a shittier than shit feeling.

But let me tell you something, as I write this, in the cold light of day I can see how unhelpful thinking that way was. And I can see that those thoughts were a load of bullshit my brain made up. I can see now that it made sense that I would feel that way. It makes sense for anyone to feel that way. Those are natural human reactions. But it's bollocks.

Children deserve to be loved. They deserve to be loved ideally by their parents. Some parents are not capable of loving their children, some parents choose not to love their children. This is NEVER the child's fault. This is NEVER because of anything the child has done. This is their problem, their shit, their issue, they are the ones with the problem. It is NEVER the fault of the child. It was never your fault!!

I did nothing wrong. My sisters did nothing wrong. There was nothing wrong with any of us. He chose to leave us because he had problems. Because he was a dickhead. Because he couldn't hack being an adult.

His fault.

His issues.

Not mine!

Bloody hell, if only I'd had that realisation at eight years old. Perhaps I would've been nicer to myself. I know I would have been nicer to myself. But what's done is done. There is no time machine, no way to go back and rewrite the story. I can only change the ending from this point on.

Always trying to comfort the inner child

I didn't really think about the term 'inner child' until I became a counsellor. Nowadays, for me, it's such a common thing for me to see and to talk about.

Every client I see is actually two people – the adult I see in front of me and the child inside them that's usually in a shit load of pain but can't work out what to do with it or how to heal it, because 9 times out of 10 they don't even realise they have an inner child. But we do, we all do. I've carried around a very hurt, bruised, confused little girl in me all my life, and every day she was asking me 'what did I do wrong?' 'why am I not loveable? 'why do people leave me'. I can almost hear her little voice; so lost, so confused, so unhappy. But do you know what I did to her for about twenty or so years before I realised she was there? I punished her. I beat her up. I slapped her in the face over and over again. I was a complete and utter bitch to her every single day. I made that broken little girl sob, I made her binge eat, I made her throw up, I starved her, I called her every evil name I could think of – monster, fat bitch, useless, pointless, miserable, pathetic, and more, so many more horrible words. I battered the poor little thing within an inch of her life, and I let others batter her too.

I failed her.

She needed compassion. She needed to be loved. She needed to be told it was never her fault. She was crying out every single day to just be loved, just be enough, just be worthy, just be held and comforted. But I didn't do any of that because I didn't even see that she was there, that she was taking that beating, but she was. And she took it, she took it for years, that little girl is strong as an ox but she almost broke. I almost killed her. I got to the point where I hated myself so much, hated everything about myself, I believed I was unlovable, believed I was worth nothing and believed that everyone would just leave me anyway because no one would want me. And I nearly killed her. I would stockpile the paracetamols; I would close my eyes for far too long while driving and I would walk into roads without looking. I wanted a way out, I looked for a way out, but I never had the courage to do it. I interpreted that as just another failure too – haven't even got the bottle to kill myself – no wonder no one wants me, of course I'm useless, of course I'm single, of course I'm fat, because I'm a rejected kid, if my own father can't love me then clearly I'm a useless waste of space.

What a waste of my life that was!! What a sad, sad, tragic waste of my life. Each thought I had like that, each time I put myself down, each time I told myself (and believed) an absolute pile of utter bollocks I wasted my life, and I was beating my inner child to death.

Please don't make my mistakes, and if you have done what I have done because you didn't know you had an inner child inside you please don't be mad at yourself. You can't know what you don't know. But please, promise me, you'll stop it. You'll look in the mirror and look into your eyes, deep into those eyes, the same eyes you've had since you were a little girl – the part of you that never changes – look into your eyes and say these few things;

"(your name), I'm so proud of you for making it through every single day to this point.

I'm so proud of you for enduring so much.

I'm so proud of you that you've done whatever has needed to be done to survive.

I'm so sorry for anything horrible I ever said to you. I didn't know the harm I was doing.

I promise you that from this point on I will look after you. I will build you up, I will compliment you, I will sing your praises, I will be proud of you and your strength and I will always be your best friend and your protector.

I love you."

What was that like? Did you do it? Did it feel weird? Or did you feel good? Like something released, something sighed, something shifted. If you did, if you felt that something softened and breathed a sigh of relief then let me tell you it did. I can tell you what you felt was you, your inner child, the little you, saying "Thank you – I've needed to hear that for so long".

FAMILY DUTY AND ALL THAT BOLLOCKS

Now, this one is going to be very different for all of us. Depending on where we live, our own cultures, our own family traditions, our family circumstances. It will all be different. However, I think a lot of us will encounter some form of conflict around duty.

It might show up in *you* first, or it might get shoved in your face by other people.

For me, it was shoved in my face by other people. By my dad's family. And this part of the story, I think, will show you just how lucky sometimes we can be to have been cast out by these men. If they come from families like mine, then you are one hundred and fifty million percent better off out of it. Seriously, you are.

So, my dad decided to die on the Monday night. He was found by the police in the house he was working in after family members had expressed concerns that they hadn't heard from him.

Monday night, my dad's family, when they got the news, wanted to ring my half-sister, who was just sixteen years old at the time, and tell her over the phone. Tell her over the phone that her dad, who'd actually been there for her for her whole sixteen years, was now dead. WTF?? Over the phone?! Seriously?? We didn't even know at that point where she was or who she was with. This was my first inkling that this family I haven't had a chance to get to know are, in fact, a bit weird.

So, Tuesday came, and the family had now given their heads a bit of shake and realised that actually it was probably best if someone told her in person. No fucking shit sherlock!

So, by a strange old twist of fate and circumstances, I somehow ended up going on a 3-hour car journey with a cousin I have only seen once in the last twenty-eight years to tell my half-sister, (that to be honest I don't really know all that well either) that our dad is dead. Fan-fucking-tastic. This is where being a bereavement counsellor went totally against me because people started to assume that I knew what to do in all circumstances surrounding death, when in fact I didn't. This was a whole new experience for me.

Anyway, I went along, she was given the news, and it was brutal. One of the worst days of my life.

But that part of duty *I chose* though and was OK with. For me, it was the right thing to do. The human thing.

The next element of duty was not OK, and it pissed me right off.

You see, once the news had been given, people started to think about the funeral. It was the Wednesday in fact, that my dad's family's thoughts turned to the funeral and the big question of who was going to pay for it.

This is where it gets messy in *lots* of families, regardless of whether the deceased is a wanker or not. It just gets messy when grieving people and money collide.

So, at this point my dad is still in the morgue, hasn't had his post-mortem, no death certificate has been issued so no one can actually even access his bank accounts to see what the situation was. (Because he's always been an absolute nob though it was a fair assumption that they would be empty. We weren't wrong, there was about £20 and just a shit load of debt to sort out.)

However, people started talking money anyway and a wonderful little Facebook messenger group was set up by some cousins that I don't even know or have had any contact with in the last twenty-eight years, and my sisters and I were added to it. The group was rather frankly & coldly called 'arrangements'.

I can feel my piss starting to boil, even just thinking about this group.

So, messages proceeded to be put in there about what was going to happen and who was going to pay.

This is where duty reared its ugly head.

You see, to my cousins, it was mine and my sisters' *duty* to pay towards this funeral and to help arrange it.

This, if you are pre-funeral is where you need to protect yourself and protect your sanity.

DO NOT HAVE SOMEONE ELSES IDEA OF DUTY INFLICTED UPON YOU!!!!!

If you *choose* to contribute, then that's fine, that's your choice; you do what you need to do. If you are official next of kin, then that is a different matter and there will be things that legally will fall on you to sort out sadly, and that's a separate kind of duty, and can't be helped.

But please do not let someone force their ideas of duty on you. Especially not now! Especially when you're in shock, processing what's just happened, and in a really weird and shitty place of complicated grief.

You were in fact abandoned by this man and you owe him NOTHING!!!

I repeat – YOU OWE HIM NOTHING.

The whole, "But, he's still your dad" bollocks, is exactly that – bollocks. Yes, biologically he's your father, but that doesn't give him the right to abandon you and then expect you to pay for his funeral. Sod that!

This is a very hard concept to get across to some people. My dad's family were spreading shite around Facebook like 'at the end of the day, family is everything' and telling the world what a beautiful, gentle soul my dad was, and that they were sorry he was dead. Then in the next breath suggesting we donate his body to medical science to save a few quid, and just scrap the idea of a funeral totally because it was too expensive to move his body and just have a piss up at one of their houses instead.

The contradictions were never ending.

My opinion was this, 'If you thought he was such a fucking beautiful soul and family is everything to you, then you pay for his funeral. Because as far as I'm concerned, and my experience of him, is that he's actually a selfish wanker who *chose* not to be my family. So, you can fucking well jog right on if you think I'm paying one single penny towards his funeral.'

Because actually, where was the family when he left my mam? Left us penniless and in shit loads of debt?..........fucked basically. Family didn't seem to be everything then, when there were three living children to look after. But suddenly family is everything when a fucking lying selfish bastard decides to die without making any provisions for his own funeral.

Fuck off!

That's not how family works in my world and if that's how you lot operate then thank fuck I got out when I was eight.

As it turned out. The money for the most basic of funerals was provided in the end by my dad's family. And I mean basic – like delivered to the crematorium basically and that's it. No service, no flowers, no nothing. The family were prepared to allow my half-sister to actually have no funeral service, just 40 minutes in the crematorium with the coffin to 'say her goodbyes'.

That wasn't acceptable to me, or my other two sisters. So, out of duty, our own sense of duty to a grieving child, we decided to put our own shit aside and attend. My sisters rallied what friends of his they could find to also attend. Songs were sent to the funeral director to have played and basically they cobbled together what we could to make it look like something resembling a funeral. The funeral director – Sean Crilly in Carlisle – was amazing, and he went above and beyond to make the whole thing look less shite and a bit more like a 'proper' funeral. The sort Scarlet has seen before and would be expecting.

Only one other member of my dad's family actually attended, and she walked into the chapel drinking her Starbucks. I could've punched her in the face. Who walks into a fucking funeral drinking a Starbucks?! Maybe you do, but I sure as shit don't, and if anyone does that at my funeral I'm coming back and haunting you!!

Duty means something different to everyone. Just please make sure you stick to what, if anything, you feel is *your* duty.

Don't be forced to attend the funeral if you don't want to. Or contribute to the cost if you don't want to.

You owe him nothing. Nothing at all. And if anyone doesn't like it then they can absolutely well and truly piss right off!

THE FUNERAL

What an absolute joke the funeral ended up being. In my head I always imagined that when he finally did die, his side of the family would arrange a funeral and my sisters and I would make the decision of whether or not we turned up. If I did attend, I imagined I would sit inconspicuously at the back and sneak out at the end before anyone noticed. That was how I'd pictured it most of the time. Occasionally, in my head, there was an almighty fight and kick off in the middle of the service as I finally aired all my thoughts about how shit he was and how shit his family were for abandoning us. Turns out none of those happened.

The money thing was an issue. Basically no one it seemed particularly liked him enough to want to contribute towards his funeral

My sisters and I owed him nothing, we didn't have to do anything – we didn't have to turn up. But actually, I think we all needed to say our goodbyes too.

The funeral was a complete and utter shambles though to be fair.

I was holding it together OK until the committal. The crematorium had this weird net curtain thing that went around the coffin as the music was playing. I don't know what the song was. Apparently, it was one of his favourites. How would I know though?

As the net went around the coffin, I noticed it had a hole in it, and that's when my thoughts started. Damn my pesky thoughts!!

They went something like this…

There's a hole in that net. They should probably sort that out. Seems kind of disrespectful to have a hole in the net. I don't know this song. It means nothing to me. I've never heard it before. I suppose he must've liked it. How would I know? There's no name plate on that coffin. I remember my granda's did. His funeral was lovely. It broke my heart to see his gorgeous name on a shiny coffin name plate. The coffin looks bigger than my granda's though. That's because my dad was tall. I remember he was so tall. Yes, he was tall. My dad was tall. My dad is in that coffin.

MY DAD IS IN THAT COFFIN!!!!!!!!!!!!!'

And that was the moment the pain hit me like an absolute train, and my eight-year-old inner child tried to take over me like a demon possessed. I actually thought I was going to explode.

BREATHE!
Keep the fuck together!!!!!!!!
BREATHE!
You're showing yourself up here.
BREATHE!
For fuck sake!
BREATHE!!!!

Oh man, I wanted to scream. I wanted to sob. I wanted to bang on the coffin and scream and shout at the bastard. I wanted to cry, scream, heave with sadness but I couldn't. It wasn't my place apparently. The funeral was for Scarlet, not me. Poor old fucking Scarlet. The one who'd actually had him as a dad for sixteen years. Yeah, let's all concentrate on her, let's all hold her and tell he it will be OK. Let's all look after her.

Who the fuck looked after me?!

Who held me night after night when I cried myself to sleep over a man who fucked off and left me?? Over a dad who couldn't be arsed?? Who looked after me and told me it would be OK when I was wetting the bed still at ten years old because I was so fucking sad?? Who the fuck looked after me??

When is that child ever going to be heard?
Be held?
Be soothed?
Be looked after?
Fuck knows.

Fucking hell those thoughts were brutal!

Half of me walked into that funeral as a thirty-six year old woman. A mum, a sister, a counsellor. But half of me walked in as an eight year old child. A sad, angry, confused eight-year-old child. And no-one held my hand. No-one told me it would be OK. No-one allowed me to be hurt, to be so desperately hurt, that I thought my heart would break into a thousand pieces as it was wrenched out of my chest and heaved up through my throat.

There was no permission to be, and to feel, exactly what I was. This is England after all, and we don't really do howling and sobbing in public very well. Especially at the funeral of a man I didn't even know – that would be totally inappropriate. And that was the problem…. I had to be pretend – bottle – wear the mask. Because after all, it was all about Scarlet wasn't it.

There was no privacy for me to mourn.

There was no permission to grieve.

Not for me.

Not at the funeral.

If you can even call it a funeral.

It was shit.

WATCH OUT FOR NIGHT-TIME

What is it about the night that brings the saddest thoughts? It's like the sky turns black and my thoughts and feelings follow it.

Another wave.

Another sad, angry, painful wave hits. While I'm washing up of all things.

The kids are just chattering upstairs. My partner isn't home yet. The dog is quiet. So, there's a gap in distraction for the hurt to find its way in.

I'm tired of it...

Frustrated with it.

Had enough of it.

These feelings have been in my life longer than he was. Fuck off feelings, you're getting on my nerves.

What am I worth if my own father didn't even love me?

These feelings always hit me at night. I think that's why I've always been a person who goes to bed early, and I never have issues getting to sleep. Because I just cannot bare to be alone with my thoughts on a night-time. My night-time thoughts are never nice ones. They never have been. They have always been the sad thoughts, and the thoughts that always focussed on why.

Why did he leave?

Why didn't he want to be around his own children?

What did we do?

What did I do?

Why can't he just come back and tell us what's going on?

Why do all my friends have dads that love them?

Why can't I just have a normal life, like everyone else?

Why doesn't he want to know me?

Those thoughts are pure heart killers. They are the ones that sting my

25

eyes, that create a huge ball in my throat, and just break me. I have no clue why. I've never known why.

It just is what has always been. This is my story. This will always be my story.

It's only now, as I write this book. As I experience these things. As I look back on my life. And as I see how my life has unfolded, I think that this was always meant to be my life. This shitty journey had a purpose, and that purpose was to help others through similar shit. So they don't lie awake at night torturing themselves with not only these thoughts, but extra ones now about why am I crying? Why am I bothered? Why can't I just switch off my emotions.

You can't do that because you're human. Because you have feelings and because this awful, shitty, complicated grief we go through is just crap.

But we aren't crap.

We aren't unlovable.

We didn't do anything wrong.

We are the innocent victims in this story.

But we are powerful. Much more powerful than the dads who decided to leave us. Who couldn't handle parenthood for whatever reason. We are the ones that will learn from this experience, will grow, and will rise stronger than we were before to help others.

That will be the legacy these men, completely by accident, leave behind.

THOSE PESKY FRIGGING 'SHOULDS'

These rear their ugly heads all the time whenever anyone dies. These are one of the biggest causes of people getting stuck in their grief and coming to me as a bereavement counsellor. Not because they have 'failed' or aren't coping, or any such bollocks like that. It's the 'Shoulds' and 'Shouldn'ts' inflicted by other people that cause problems. They prevent people from processing their loss in the way that they need to in order to heal. So, these are a total nightmare when it comes to bereavement generally but brace yourself because you're going to hear these all the time when it's a dead absent father!

You'll probably hear at least one, if not all of these;
You *should* be crying....
You *shouldn't* be crying....
You *should* be bothered....
You *shouldn't* be bothered....
You *should* go to the funeral......
You *shouldn't* go to the funeral.......
You *should* go to work....
You *shouldn't* go to work....
You *should* view the body....
You *shouldn't* view the body....

Blah, blah, blah, endless lists of them!!
Urgh!! Fuck off!!
The only thing you should or shouldn't be doing is what feels right for you!
You are the expert in you!

27

You know how to heal yourself from this shitty, horrible, confusing mess.

Listen to yourself and yourself only. And give everyone else's shoulds and shouldn'ts a big fat kick up the arse!!

ANGER

Oh, the anger!!!!

After the initial phone call and the bit of crying that night, the anger came. It came with a bang. It came like a big fucking train with flashing lights and lots of noise. It wanted to be seen. It *needed* to be seen. It needed to be heard. It stamped its feet like the eight-year-old child never could, and it threw the mother fucker of all tantrums. It was like a furnace rose from the depths of my soul and some weird, angry beast was unleashed. I didn't give a shit who saw it, what it said, or who it fired its flames of wrath at. Look out world Wendy was on the warpath!

It was exhausting.

Because what could I actually do with that anger really??

The twat is already dead, so I can't do anything to him.

I don't want to go to prison, so going and beating the shit out of the insensitive cousins that very quickly started to piss me off wasn't actually going to happen.

And annoyingly, I'm actually quite a wimp. I hate confrontation. I'm an introvert by nature. So, I did what any self-respecting introvert does – I started writing!

I started writing what's now become this book. I started writing poetry (I'm such a moody poet, I only ever do it when I'm pissed off or heartbroken), I wrote a few ranty (ish - they weren't too bad I suppose) Facebook posts, and then sent the mother of all messages into that shitty Facebook messenger group.

But then what?

It didn't really seem like that was enough. Like the anger had been purged from my soul properly.

It was at that point that I again happened to have another luxury you might not have reading this.

As counsellors we need to have regular supervision. Every month, we go and discuss anything that might be concerning us with our practice. Has a client got under our skin? Do we feel stuck? Do we need some support ourselves? It's a way of keeping both client and counsellor safe, and my God was I grateful I had Julie that week!

I ranted and raved at her; told her how pissed off I was – how much my dad's family had pissed me off. Just how fucking pissed off I was generally.

But then I mentioned the weird thing about thinking I'd seen him in Tesco, and how actually, I'd been seeing loads of people that looked like him – tall, thin, grey haired men with beards and glasses - and my heart leaping out of my chest because I thought it was him.

And this is where the anger gave way to something else. Something much worse.

Pain & sadness.

Heart wrenching, lump in the throat making, eyes on fire kind of pain.

She saw it – I felt it – we both knew it was there. And she said, 'be careful, anger is a much easier emotion to identify, but it's usually just a mask for something more painful.'

Yep – nail on head Julie – 10 out of 10.

Anger had always been acceptable in my life. Anger hid everything for years. It was OK to scream and shout, slam doors, fight with my sisters, (well, kind of, my mam probably didn't find it that acceptable). But It's a lot easier to get angry than admit I was sad and in emotional pain. It was easier to call him the twat, the wizard, the nob head etc etc, and to be angry about it. It's a lot harder to say, "You know what? It really hurts that my dad didn't want me. It feels shit every single day and makes me feel like I'm unlovable. I would've really loved a dad."

Man, even writing that stings like a bitch – I can't see the keys on the laptop for tears. For fuck sake! The bastard is even in the way now!

Yep, anger is much, much, much more comfortable.

WEIRD SPOOKY SHIT

Pretty much every person I have supported through their bereavement has had a 'spooky' story. Sometimes its signs; they feel they've had a sign from the deceased – a feather, a robin, a flower – could be anything really. Sometimes they've actually seen the person, heard the person, sensed the person in some way. Or, they've had a dream where they've felt sure they were actually visited by the person. Sometimes objects have moved in the house, lost items have reappeared, or just something really weird and unexplainable has happened.

When people have sheepishly told me their stories, they usually start it with "you're going to think I'm mad but............", I always look at them and smile and say, "If I wasn't already a believer in the weird and wonderful I would absolutely have to be now – you can't all be going mad surely! It seems everyone I speak to has a story like yours."

Phew!!! Is the usual response to that!

It's true though, just about everyone seems to have one. And the ones that don't share a 'spooky' story I'm pretty sure just haven't dared to say it.

So, don't panic. Don't think you're suddenly ready for your local mental hospital if you see, hear, or sense something. There is so much we just don't understand about death. And nobody has a clue what happens, so if you feel that you get a message or sign or whatever, then own it as being whatever you think it is, because no one can actually prove otherwise.

Yes, you've guessed it, I have my own weird story about my dead dad.

A few days after he died, I was having one of those awful hurt moments. Where I was sobbing those big heavy ugly tears – although on this occasion I was in bed and I was trying not to wake up my partner, so the tears were actually a bit more painful because I was trying to keep them

31

in a bit. I was angry this particular night too and somehow my mind wandered to the thoughts of spookiness and whether he would try and 'haunt' me.

I remember shouting at him in my head – along the lines of "You were never there! Never made a fucking effort! Never stepped up!"

Rant rant rant, swear word followed swear word......

"So, don't even fucking think about tipping up as a fucking ghost when you couldn't even be arsed to visit when you were alive!! Twat – wanker – arsehole – nobhead etc etc.

And then came my own spooky experience.

I heard his voice.

It was an actual voice – in my ear – not in my head like a memory of a voice. And I could feel a presence so close to my face. Sort of like when you're at the opticians and they get really close. You know they aren't touching you, but you can feel the closeness of their head right next to yours. It was like that.

I know I was shocked. I know my heart beat fifty to the dozen. But I wasn't scared.

I can't remember what the frig he said though which is hugely annoying! I'm sure he said "goodnight", but I think he said something else too. Why can't I remember? You'd think I would remember. For whatever reason I don't though. Who knows why that is. Certainly not me.

I was also pretty annoyed in the morning though. Of course I was, I think you're getting to realise I can be quite an angry person!

I was annoyed because I've never heard the voices of my gran or granda. People who I loved so much, and who I knew loved me. I get signs from them often, and I sense their protection and influence, but I've never heard their voice. And I would love to hear them. However, just writing this now, it's just dawned on me that I still can't watch videos with them in or read the book my granda used to read me because I'll hear his voice in my head and I simply can't bare it yet. So, penny just dropped there, I'm not ready to hear their voices, and they knew that before it clicked in my brain. That's why they haven't.

So, don't worry about weird shit happening. And don't worry if you suddenly start an interest in going to see a medium when you'd never believed in all that before. It's all part of searching for answers, and it's totally natural.

OTHER WEIRD SHIT HAPPENING IN YOUR BRAIN

As I wrote the last chapter about weird spooky shit, I remembered another weird thing that my brain was doing. In fact, it was doing it pretty often, especially after the funeral.

Weird dreams.

Weird 'flashbacks'

Weird old memories regurgitating.

The dreams were usually about post-mortems, funerals, death in general. They were pretty unpleasant but not really all that much of a worry.

It was the weird flashbacks and old memories that were a strange shock. I think it was to do with photos and old faces. There were lots of photos flying around and my sister posted one particular photo on Facebook that caused my brain no end of misery. It was a photo of my dad back in the 1990s wearing his leather biker jacket. That was how I remembered him as a child. That tall, slim, bearded man with dark hair and aviator style glasses and his biker jacket. It's amazing how one photo can transport your mind back in time so far and be so vivid. It was like a computer suddenly uploading and opening an old file full of more photos that were just popping up on the screen. The screen being my memories and my mind. I could remember things from childhood, not that many things, but snapshots of my dad being around. Most of it was boring, mundane or unpleasant. I remembered him chasing me up the stairs to smack me one time when we were on holiday somewhere. I remember he burned my chin with his fag as he zipped my coat up on a beach once. I remember him getting annoyed and being someone that you had to kind of tip toe around. The memories weren't all bad. But they were heavily weighted in that direction, and they came at me thick and fast just from seeing one little photo.

That wiped me out for a whole evening to be honest. I was no good. Just a big old emotional wreck sobbing over a photo of a man I barely knew.

The other really weird instance of this was after the funeral. If you do go to your dad's funeral and it's been a long time since you had anything to do with him, then brace yourself for random people turning up from your childhood. It will potentially send you brain into memory recall overload and it doesn't half knock the wind out of you!

My godfather turned up at the funeral. Someone who had been a relatively frequent visitor to the family when I was little, but that I'd also not seen since my dad left. I saw him in the car park and I said, 'I know you, don't I?' Then I suddenly realised who he was, and actually he looked no different. His voice was exactly the same too. Loads of memories came flooding back. It was overwhelming. It didn't feel like my brain could cope. That constant downloading of old memories continued into the early hours of that night. It was weird and exhausting, but I just let it happen. I trusted that this was something that just had to happen. I wrote some things down. I didn't try and judge or analyse any of the memories or any of the emotions that came with them. I just pretty much thanked my brain for giving me all that and let it run its course. Almost like watching a movie. There was no point in trying to stop it, press pause or rewind it. I just let it play out, then I went to sleep eventually afterwards.

Try not to judge any emotions that come to you when memories are triggered, just allow them to come and to go away again. The more you try and battle with them, I find, the longer they hang around.

THE EMPTY LOSS

I tried to explain it to my partner the other night. Tried to explain what it's like to grieve for someone you didn't know. It was the fourth anniversary of my gran's death and as I'd been driving to work that morning, I was thinking about her. I could remember her singing. I could remember her always having a cold nose, and for some reason always wanting you to feel it to see that it was actually cold, and she wasn't making it up – yep, weird I know. I remember her knitting without even looking at the knitting needles (I swear that woman was some kind of knitting superhuman). I remembered countless conversations, countless times she'd embarrassed the hell out of us in restaurants by saying something inappropriate. I remembered her coughing – that always scared the shite out of me, I always thought she'd croak. Remembered her strength and unbelievable stubbornness. And I remembered so much more. So much more. Because I *knew* her. I'd known her for thirty-two years. My whole life. And I miss her presence. I'd give anything, absolutely anything to hear her cough again and touch that bloody cold nose!! As utterly painful as it is that she's not here, grieving for her, missing her, crying and being in such pain when I think about the fact she's not here, makes total sense. It's awful, but it makes total sense in my head. I miss her and my heart breaks that she isn't here but that's how it should be. It's how I *want* it to be.

But when I think about my dad, I have literally a handful of fleeting memories. I couldn't tell you if he drank tea or coffee. I couldn't tell you what his favourite songs, TV programs, books were. I don't know if he even watched TV or read books. I don't recall any conversations really, I don't have anything to miss. There isn't an empty seat at the Christmas table because he was never there anyway. I don't miss his calls or cards on my birthday because he was never there anyway. I don't have those things to miss.

35

There's an empty grief.

I feel shattered and battered by it all – by all the emotions – by the end of hope, by the fact that he's now gone. But I have nothing to miss. No memory box, no picture to walk by and say 'I miss you' to, no memories to make the pain make sense.

Just emptiness.

Painful emptiness.

How the hell do you explain that?

How do you even make sense of that in your own head?

And what do you even do with that?

I'll be honest, I'm still working that one out.

GRIEF AMBUSHES

Grief ambushes are something that as a bereavement counsellor, I've been warning clients about for years. I have no clue where or when I first came across this phrase, I certainly didn't invent it, I don't think, but it's just such an accurate description.

Grief ambushes are basically moments when you're going about your day in a seemingly OK, non-descript, mediocre kind of way, and then all of a sudden – wallop!!!!

For no apparent reason, you're suddenly a gibbering, emotional wreck and you find yourself back in the rawness of grief. These tend to hit me while I'm driving for some bizarre reason, which is really not the safest of places to suddenly get struck with an attack of the tears!

I don't know the scientific reason as to why these happen, maybe someone somewhere does. I'm personally not interested in *why* they happen, I just know that they do, and that they're a natural part of grief.

The best explanation/analogy I've come up with so far for clients is that the death of the person is like an earthquake happening. You get the immediate devastation and fall out directly after the death, and then grief ambushes are like aftershocks/tremors. You never know when they're coming and they always last for different amounts of time and have different strengths. The best advice I've ever been able to come up with, when dealing with these ambushes/aftershocks/tremors is protect yourself and ride it out. In an earthquake after shock I guess you'd head for the doorway or under a table (we don't really have them in the UK so I am literally just going off TV here!) and you'd keep yourself as safe possible until it's time to come back out. Grief ambushes are similar. Get yourself somewhere safe, let the tears fall, the rant come out, the anger escape safely, whatever is required at that moment, and ride it out until it stops, and you can come back into 'the real world'.

If you're thinking of trying to stop these grief ambushes then good luck, the whole point of an ambush is that you don't see it coming.

If you're thinking of squashing the emotion back in and preventing the grief ambush from taking control, then good luck, it gets harder and harder each time.

Speaking from experience, when these little bastards come along, uninvited to your otherwise OK day, just let them have their moment, let whatever emotion it is that's stamping its feet for attention have it, then reapply your mascara and carry on with your day as best you can.

Seriously, I haven't found a better way than to just surrender to them, they seem to move on much quicker when you.

HEAD VS HEART – WHEN WILL I ACCEPT THEY'RE GONE?

I see a lot of bereaved people in my job, and one of the things that pops up time and time again is this idea of *acceptance*. There's an idea that grief runs a nice path, in stages, from shock to acceptance. You might have come across the 'stages of grief' theories. I'm not the biggest fan of those approaches to bereavement to be honest. Yes, there are similarities between us all when we are bereaved, most of us will feel shock, denial, anger, will try bargaining, searching etc but they certainly don't go in any sort of pattern and we certainly don't all experience all of them. Bereavement is a totally unique thing, and it can cause people a lot of unnecessary upset if they then start worrying that they are not 'grieving properly' because they haven't personally experienced stage number 3 or whatever. Acceptance means different things to different people and I always talk about two levels of acceptance with my clients. The head will accept the death in one way, and at one time. And the heart will accept it in another way, at another time. Almost always, the head is the quickest. It's the bit that says 'yep, they're definitely dead (because either they trust the people who've told them or they've seen the body) and 'yep they're definitely dead because I've been to the funeral' – that's the logical part of yourself processing the loss and accepting that yes, in fact this person is now actually dead.

But the heart often does something different. It does things to a person that look like this;

'Maybe they (the police, mortuary, coroner etc) got it wrong? Maybe they got the wrong name, and it wasn't him'

'It just doesn't *feel* real'

'I can't even cry about it, it can't be true if I'm not even crying'

'I keep searching for them'

'I keep hoping that one day they'll walk through the door'
'I just can't believe that they're really gone'

Hearts tend to be the slowest. Personally, I think that only when brain and heart meet, is where any true acceptance comes, and it tends to come in painful bursts. That's the bit that people are usually the most afraid of. Because it does hurt. When your heart is accepting something and feeling the pain of it, it really really really hurts. Clients will say things to me like 'I actually feel real pain in my chest, like I can't breathe, like I'm being crushed and will explode', and they're so worried and frightened about it, and think it's not normal and sadly, the only 'comfort' I can give them, is yes, it is normal, it is natural, but it's called being heartbroken and that term exists for a reason – and that's because heart ache, and heart break is in fact very very real and it hurts like hell. Emotions are not some wishy washy experience that only hormonal teenagers get – they are powerful forces to be respected, protected and acknowledged. When the emotional pain of grief comes your way you'd better brace yourself because its bringing a power your way that can, and does, literally knock people to the ground, that breaks their heart, that rips the very breath from their lungs, that affects their bladder and bowels, that rocks you to your very core. And it hurts! It hurts like fuck and it keeps hurting, it keeps hurting until it's healed. And the one sure thing with bereavement is that it will always leave a scar. There will always be a tiny bit that can't be fully healed, because it will never be OK. In cases where you loved a person, it's never OK that they're gone. It will never be OK for me that my grandparents aren't here anymore – never. For the rest of my life I know full well that I will miss them. I will think about them, and I would give anything I have to see them one more time; to talk to them one more time, and hug them just one more time. My heart will never be OK with the fact they're gone because I so desperately wish they weren't. I can accept it, yes, but with great pain. But it will never ever be OK.

For us with the twat dads, it's different I suppose. It is for me at least. I don't really want to see him one more time, to have one more conversation. I don't think I'd actually want it, and if there was ever a choice between seeing my grandparents once more or my dad, I would choose my grandparents. But there is still a bit of a battle going on between head and heart, but because my heart had been so far removed from my dad for so many years, it just feels really hard to work out which is which. My heart only really knows feelings of loss, rejection, pain, sadness, confusion when it comes to my dad anyway. I feel like I got a head start on the heart part, because I've been grieving his loss already for twenty-eight years. If anything, it's my head that needs to catch up, it's definitely the one having issues with this one.

In all honesty, some people never fully accept that someone has gone and personally I'm OK with that. I'm not into forcing people to 'grieve properly', it's a term that makes my piss boil to be perfectly honest because I think it's a load of bullshit and is totally patronising. There is no rule book on how to grieve. You grieve however you bloody well need to. You heal the best you can to be able to live your life, but that can look 7 billion different ways for each person on the planet as far as I'm concerned. If you need to pretend someone has just been on holiday for years and years and that's why they haven't come back, then you do that!

Do what you need to do. Go with your own instincts and your own flow. Heal in the way you need to heal. Let go of the idea that you are meant to grieve in a 'one size fits all' way, because it just doesn't happen that way, it really doesn't.

I NEEDED A GRAVE, SO I BORROWED ONE

Before my dad died, my grandparents died. All four of them in fact. I never knew my paternal grandfather, and my paternal grandmother - 'Granny at Peterlee' - I only knew until I was ten years old. I have some lovely memories of her, but she also scared me a little bit. She was a lot older than my other gran and she was a hugger and a kisser. That freaked me out a bit as a child. I wasn't from an otherwise 'huggy' family. And she was old and wrinkly, and for a child that can just be a bit freaky. I loved her, I loved visiting her home, the memories are fond, but scarce. When she died, I was sad, and I dare say I grieved in my own way, but I don't really remember much to be honest.

My other grandparents, my mam's parents, were the best. They took us all over the place, babysat us all the time. We must've stayed at their house more than our own sometimes. They were there at everything. They were the jackpot of grandparents and I was incredibly lucky to have my gran with me for thirty-two years and my granda for thirty-four. When they died my world came crashing down and I felt pain that I'd never experienced before. Grief does weird, weird things to a person. I struggled. Really struggled.

I'll often explain to my bereavement clients that bereavement is like being blasted into a million pieces but somehow you survived the blast. The pieces not only have to come back together and heal but they have to come back and at the same time create a whole new version of you. That process is painful, confusing, takes time and is exhausting. I had to learn to be a person that now had no grandparents in the physical world at all. That version of me was brand new and to be honest the pieces still haven't come back together yet, perhaps they never will.

This is where listening to your inner voice comes in and is so important. The pieces must fall back into place in a way that suits you. It's such a personal, unique thing. You can't follow another person's way of grieving –

42

it just won't work.

Without realising it probably, you will, right from the start, be telling yourself what you need to do to heal. Learn to start listening and don't be surprised if they come at you disguised as pretty weird ideas!

My grandparents were both cremated and my mam, for some bizarre reason, chose to just have their ashes scattered at the crematorium. Cheers mam. For her, having a 'memorial place' was not important for her healing process. Up until that point, I hadn't felt it was that important either.

However, when both grandparents were gone, my heart was crying out for a grave, or a place to remember them – just somewhere to go. But there wasn't one. It kept coming to my mind all the time - "I need a grave – I need a grave". It was really bugging me to be honest because I knew there wasn't one.

Then, one day, I remembered two things. One was going with my grandparents to the cemetery down the road from their house. My gran's parents and sister were buried there, and she used to regularly lay flowers there. And the second thing I remembered, was my granda, after my gran died, taking flowers there too on her behalf.

Bingo! Penny dropped.

It was at that point that I knew what I had to do. I cut some white roses from the rosebush in my garden one Sunday morning and I went in search of that grave. I knew where the cemetery was but hadn't been for about twenty years. I didn't have a clue which grave it was. Thankfully I found it really quickly and easily.

I went to that grave with fresh flowers every month for around eighteen months. I borrowed that grave, and I knelt there and wept. I spoke to them all there, each member of my dead family. It became like a sort of communal grave. I made the flowers look nice and I remembered them all. I felt close to them, and I knew my gran would be grateful that I was doing that for her.

To someone else, this would have sounded bizarre;

'You're going to put flowers on a grave that isn't even your grandparents to feel closer to your grandparents?! Eh?? WTF?!'

You can just imagine the comments, can't you?! But it worked for me. Each month it worked, it helped the pieces find a way back together, and it helped me to heal. Not a clue how, but it worked.

I haven't been now for months, but I don't beat myself up about that, it never *had* to be something I did forever. It worked at that moment in time, and now at *this* moment in time I don't feel I need to go there. Who knows though, in the future I might, and that's OK too.

Go with your gut, do what you need to do. You know how to heal yourself. Trust your intuition.

When it comes to healing from my dad's loss, it seems writing has been my medicine. There's no rule that says you need to use the same medicine to heal from each loss.

BEING PRESENT IN MY OWN GRIEF

I've worked with so many people who are bereaved. I wouldn't even be able to tell you how many. And it's tough work. Brutal work. It's the work that for me has always been the most painful. As a counsellor you are exposed to pain and suffering on a daily basis, you look it in the eye and you try and feel the full force of it, so you can properly empathise with your client. A counsellor's job is to see life from your point of view and help you to understand it. That means we dive in. We dive into the deepest waters that you are in and we feel it as much as we can. Our job is not to dive in and get lost with you, we have to keep one foot on safe ground, to keep you safe. But we can't just stand on the side lines either, we have to dive in. In my experience there are no deeper, choppier, colder, more frightening waters than the pain of bereavement. It's rough. It's powerful. And It can feel unrelenting. Stepping, voluntarily into a raging sea of pain is a difficult task, and any counsellor who says it doesn't affect them, is either not doing their job properly or lying. It does affect you. It affects me. I have sobbed for my clients. I have felt heartbroken for my clients. And I have regularly felt completely and utterly useless. When it comes to bereavement there are no therapeutic goals to work towards, there are no tasks you can suggest to the client to help change their situation. All you can do is dive in, hold on tight and reassure them as much as possible that one of two things are going to happen – they are either going to become very able to ride out these storms as they become more familiar with them, or the storm is gradually going to ease off. It very much depends which grief model you get on board with. Either way, it's quite a journey into a client's pain. It's a tough journey, but for me, it's some of the most rewarding and fulfilling work I do.

I wouldn't say that doing this work has made anything any easier when

I've been bereaved, although it has prepared me in a way. It's given me a lot of familiarity with death, bereavement and grief.

I had the benefit of realising right from the start that I was in very choppy and unfamiliar waters. My emotions were all over the place. It was horrible, it was painful, it was shit of epic proportions, but I was strangely present in my own grief. I knew what was going on. I recognised all the 'symptoms' and part of me sort of watched myself grieving with fascination. It almost felt in a way like I was a counsellor to myself. Which actually really helped. I could talk things through with myself in a more rational way. I knew I wasn't mentally ill so I didn't have that to worry about, and I knew that at some point the feelings would change into something else and I'd just deal with whatever came my way without any judgement.

It was a strange experience and I'm sure any other counsellors who pick up this book might have had similar experiences. I was lucky to have this element, and I feel like it's really helped me to heal and not become stuck emotionally.

I'M NOT ALLOWED TO CRY

That was the message about my dad leaving right from the start really. My sister told me straight away the night my mam told us he wasn't going to live with us anymore, not to cry over him, he wasn't worth it. And I don't remember my sisters ever crying, about anything – ever. Or my mam. It just wasn't something that happened in my house. Anger we were all very open with, but sadness and crying, no, not so much.

And then, somehow the world gave me the same message – don't cry, he's not worth it.

My friends would give me that message, it seems like that was just the standard message.

And I suppose living in England doesn't really help. Stiff upper lip keep calm and carry on, and all that bollocks. It's kind of ingrained in us to not cry about stuff, just move on, forget about it, stop making a fuss, just deal with it.

And I suppose I did deal with it. I learned to cry quietly. In secret. That worked. And I learned that it just wasn't going to get talked about, not really, not properly, not how I needed it to be. So I just got on with my life as best as I could. Dragging around a great big black pain with me wherever I went. Dragging this big black pain into every friendship, every relationship, into every day. It just seemed to hang there on my heart, squashing it and stopping me from seeing the good stuff that was all around me.

The message to not cry carried on after he was dead too.

'Don't cry, why are you bothered'

'Don't cry, you've got nothing to cry about, you didn't even know him'

'Don't cry, this isn't as bad for you as it is for Scarlet'

'Don't cry, what's the point'

'Don't cry, you'll look an idiot'

47

'Don't cry, don't cry, don't cry............well do you know what, I needed to fucking cry. I needed to scream and wail and sob, I needed to purge that big black pain from myself like a ginormous shite! It needed to fucking go, because I had dragged that bastard around with me for twenty-eight years and to be honest, I was sick of it – sick of the feel of it – the weight of it – the influence it had – the way it got in the way of everything. That big black pain made me feel like I wasn't enough, wasn't loveable, wasn't good enough, wasn't the same as everyone else, could never have what they had. It wore me down. Every single frigging day it wore me down and I had had enough. It was time for it to go.

But then, the unexpected happened..............I didn't want to let it go. I didn't want to be without that big black pain because it was familiar, it was part of me, it was part of my identity. I don't like change generally, and this would be a big big change. If I let this go, then I would be different, and I wasn't sure I was ready or able to be that kind of different. To not have that pain.

Weird I know, bizarre even, but that's just how it was.

But you know, somehow, I did get rid of it, I search for it now and I can't find it. That blackness, that pain, that old idea that I just mustn't be good enough because my dad didn't love me is just not there anymore.

Somehow, through the sobbing, the wailing, the writing since he's died. I've purged that big black rock from my heart.

I can feel the difference.

It wasn't some massive lightning bolt experience, there was no obvious outward change in my appearance. There was no fanfare and applause. I just feel different.

Lighter,

Less burdened,

More peaceful,

Calmer.

Those things haven't come overnight, it's been a gradual process over the last twenty-eight years, but now I suppose I've been able to get that old chestnut cliché – closure.

His death brought the end of the suffering of hope. Hope was the thing that set me up for disappointment over and over again. Even though logical me knew he was never going to change, emotional me was holding onto that hope with an iron grip. Emotional me was winning the battle without me even realising.

Now, emotional me has had to listen to logic and the two levels of acceptance have come together – head and heart in perfect union. He's dead, you're never having the dad you always wanted, logic and emotion both agree.

So, I'm left with acceptance. But acceptance without the mental beating of 'I'm not good enough...I wasn't loveable....I must've done something wrong....some of it at least must've been my fault'

It was that mental battering that caused me the most pain, and now that that isn't happening, my head and heart are happier. They're free from daily abuse and that's what has shrunk the big black pain. I've killed it with kindness I suppose.

The world might tell us not to cry, our families and friends might tell us not to cry, we will probably even tell ourselves not to cry, but the thing is this – if you need to cry just go and bloody well do it. Let that shit out. Freely and wholeheartedly give yourself permission to lock yourself in the bathroom, running a shower you've no intention of actually getting in just to hide the noise, and cry your fucking eyes out. As many times as you need to. If you don't have the luxury of being able to do it out in 'public' so to speak (by that, I mean among your family and friends) then just find somewhere and go and do it.

My car became my place to cry for many many years. Drive into the middle of nowhere and sob like a woman possessed. No one ever saw it, no one ever knocked on the window and asked if I was OK. No one had a clue.

Do what you need to do. But don't bottle. Don't ever bottle up this shitty stuff because it will just make you ill. It will make you bitter, it will cause you pain and at some point, will come out in some enormous shitty mess that will literally scare the shit out of you. Don't do that to yourself. Don't wait for crisis point. Release any shit regularly. I promise you you'll feel better for it.

And for anyone who tells you not to cry when he's dead because you didn't even know him in the first place, send them my way and I'll tell them to fuck right off. They don't know what it's like, they don't know the complicated, shitty emotional place we find ourselves in, so balls to them, this is our grief and we'll deal with it however the fuck we need to.

What we experience, in technical terms is disenfranchised grief. It's where we feel as though we don't have permission to grieve. People experience this in lots of ways; it could be;

- The mistress who doesn't feel she has permission to grieve because no one knew she was having an affair with the deceased.
- The person grieving the loss of their pet, because the world will say, 'it's only a dog, cat, hamster, frog'
- The person grieving for their ex-partner; the world will say 'but you'd split up, why are you bothered?'.
- The person grieving their grandparents, 'why are you upset, it's the natural way, they'd had a good innings'

It happens all the time, in so many different ways. There's an invisible, unspoken hierarchy added to grief that goes something like this;

children – spouse – parents – siblings – friends – pets

And its utter bollocks.

We miss who we miss, we grieve for whoever it is we love. And it's different for all of us.

We're people after all - all unique. We're not robot clones. Don't forget that.

LIVING WITH IT.
IT ALL CHANGED GRADUALLY - EXTRACTS FROM MY DIARY

Late September 2018

I'm not sure if all wounds can be healed. I think this one might always be open in some way, because the only person who could've maybe healed it couldn't be arsed and has now had the complete selfishness to go and fucking die.

Wanker.

(One of the first steps for me living with this was announcing it on social media. Yeah, I know, cringe. There were a few other family members posting things about how much of a 'beautiful soul', and a 'gentleman' he was that I thought, hang on, I don't fucking think so! And the rebellious part of me wanted to get my side of things out there.

Most of my friends knew he was dead and knew I was struggling, but something in me felt I needed to make some kind of public announcement).

So, I did. And this was it...

"So, my biological father died on Monday night.

Anyone who's known me since I was a kid knows that him leaving screwed me up a bit and caused me a lot of pain.

We didn't have a relationship, he sort of popped into my life every now and again (usually when he was ill) and that was it really.

I tolerated him to be honest because of my little half-sister, Scarlet. I wanted to know her.

I feel for her now because she had him as a father and she's mourning his loss as a child who had their father should

I always wondered how this day would feel, when he wasn't here anymore. I thought I wouldn't be bothered. Can't miss what you never had, right?

But I was wrong.

It's been a lot harder than I thought.

The pain and hurt from the past has hit me like a train to be honest and the realisation that I will never know why he left and continued to choose to not be interested in knowing me is really really tough.

So, I'm ranting to anyone that will listen. Drinking more than I probably should. But looking after myself in the best way that I can and trying to nurture that eight year old inner child that's mourned his loss once already.

To anyone out there, any other rejected kids whose absent parent has now died, it feels really complicated and shit doesn't it, and my heart goes out to you xx"

I have to say, people were really lovely. And a few people reached out to me to say that yes, they were rejected kids too and that they agreed it was really shit. They gave me the usual, "it gets easier with time" spiel. I don't think people know what else to say really.

But I guess they were right, because it did get easier…

10/10/2018

The funeral was on Friday and I tried to go back to work the very next Monday.

Big mistake for me. Going back to work was just too much.

Within ten minutes I'd burst into tears – big ugly tears in front of my colleagues.

Brilliant! Urgh

I'm not good with public emotion, I didn't do it all when I was young. I've learned it in the past few years since training to be a counsellor. I wouldn't be much of a counsellor if I can't allow emotion! I've learned its ok to be real. Its ok to hurt. Holding it in does no good. I've held way too much in over the years, and now it's just too big. There's nowhere left to bury it. There's no space. I have no choice now but to let it out. I feel like it needs to be purged.

To be set free.

To be released.

But who will I be without it?

Will I still be me?

A me without pain

Without hurt

Do I dare to be her?

I just don't know, and to be honest I'd rather not do all this painful soul searching in the office at work in front of all my colleagues.

I took the whole of that week off. I needed time to try and work some of this out in private.

14/10/2018

It'll be a month tomorrow since he died. Since that weird call in the night. Since the anger, the dramas, the tears. Time is such a weird thing; 4 weeks usually flies right by and feels like nothing but at the moment 4 weeks feels like forever.

I'm going back to work tomorrow. I feel prepared this time. Time to face the world again. Part of me feels ready, like its time. But part of me knows I still have healing to do. Some of the pain came out but I'm sure there's still some just lurking in the shadows. I'm going to have to choose to ignore it for now because I need to function. I need to work. I need to pay the bills. I need to feed my kids. All the strength I have now needs to go on burying the leftover emotion. I don't have space and time to deal with it just now.

I buried the pain once before when I was eight, I can do it again.

Not the healthiest approach in the world I know, but right now, its my only option.

15/10/2018

Work was OK today. It's been a month and I feel slightly calmer about everything now.

I'm very aware that there's still something lurking though. Some unfinished business. But for now, it needs to wait. I'm not ready to look at it yet. To turn that page. To face that demon. To let it go even.

Part of me needs to hold onto it. Hold onto the pain. Hold onto the drama. The chaos. Because without it, without the hurt, the pain, the sadness, the rejection…I'm not sure who I am.

I don't know how to be confident yet. To be self-assured. To have real high regard for myself.

I'm used to being rejected, to being unworthy, to being desperate for love.

I'm not sure who this person is that I'm becoming. I don't know her yet. She even scares me a little. But I'm proud as fuck of her. She's got strength that I didn't even realise was there.

Just like the quote my sister shared to my Facebook page today;

"Though she be but little, she is fierce."

03/11/18

I miss the pain.

Right now, it's just emptiness. My life, as it goes on, is actually unaffected by his death. There is nothing to miss. No one is really talking about him now, and the raw, uncontrollable emotion has passed. It's just me, and the nothingness now. No memories. Nothing to miss. Life is literally carrying on as if nothing happened. But something did happen. My dad died. He's well and truly, completely and utterly gone.

All hope is gone.

There will never be chance now to get that apology, to get those answers, to get the hugs I always wanted, to have a dad protect me. It's gone.

But the world carries on.

I carry on.

With nothing to miss.

But knowing that I missed so much.

*You have no option but to try and pretend it isn't important. To put on a brave face and tell the world 'It's ok, I had a great mum and grandparents instead', 'I was lucky he didn't stay around because he would've only messed my life up', 'you can't miss what you never had' etc etc etc. it's all bullshit. It's the story I had to say to be able to carry on. Because to go through life each day reminding myself how much it hurts to be rejected, and how much you **can** actually miss something you never had, and actually just how shite it really is, is just too hard. So, the 'its fine' story had to exist to save me.*

But it's so unbelievably not fine.

I'm not fine!

I feel like something inside of me is breaking, shattering even. I feel fragile. I feel lost. I feel like I want to go back to when he just died, to those awful strong, painful emotions. Because I felt close to him then. He was being talked about all the time, there were pictures of him and people saying things about him and I even heard his fucking ghostly voice. I felt like he was around. And now, just like before, he's not. And he's never going to be. I'm back now to that shitty place of being fatherless, although this time it's without any tiny glimmer of hope attached. He's well and truly gone. I always thought that would bring relief, it almost felt like it did at the beginning, but now it doesn't. It just creates a whole new kind of void. And my mind now needs to write a whole new script. I can't use the 'yeah, my dad doesn't really bother with me, he's off god knows where doing god knows what, but it's fine' (while holding silently to the hope that one day the version will be 'my dad came back, and we now get on really well') script anymore. Now the reality is 'my dad never cared, never came back and now he's dead'. And what the fuck do I do with that?

What can anyone do with that?

It's utterly, utterly shit. And I suppose I'm doing what I've always done. Take one day at a time. Write down the pain to get it out. Cry when I can. And just keep going. I'm not sure there's a better way for me right now.

11/11/18

At the moment I feel really numb. There's no anger raging inside me like there was. Even while some family members are still being nasty and the subject of paying for the funeral continues back and forth — everyone wanting to get out of that one — I'm only angry at their behaviour and then it goes.

It's a weird kind of emptiness.

When I think about my dad at the moment, I don't really feel anything. It doesn't feel real that he's dead. He was never really alive to me in the first place.

Yes, that makes sense — he was never really alive to me in the first place.

I noticed something this morning. I'd logged onto Instagram for the first time in about 2 weeks and my little half-sister had posted one of those moving collage photo things; all with photos of her and our dad on it. It didn't really affect me at all. It was kind of like 'oh, I wonder how you do those photo collage thingy's' rather than any hurt, any feelings, anything in relation to my dad really.

My middle sister has occasionally posted photos of my granda, and when they pop up in my newsfeed it's like a knife goes through my chest and I want to switch the phone off and look away as quickly as possible. It hurts. It reminds me he's not here anymore and the pain of missing him is just almost too much to bare. Just writing this now I can feel the pain building in my chest — a heaviness, a weight right on my lungs, and there's a sting in the back of my throat, then it hits my eyes. Yep, the eyes are leaking right now.

But that's how I want it to be. I want to feel that every time I think about my granda because I loved him, and I miss him and I would give anything to sit once more in my grandparents living room and just listen to them tell me who in the town has just died, how crap the government is, how good things were in the olden days and how many times they've been to see the doctor in the last month. I'd give anything for that. It hurts like hell, but I wouldn't swap that painful feeling, because as shit as it is, I feel lucky to have it. I feel lucky that I had such beautiful grandparents that loved me. I feel lucky to have had people in my life that I miss so much. They say that grief is the price you pay for loving someone, and as shit as it feels I'm glad I have it. I'm glad I ruin my mascara as often as I do, I'm glad my heart breaks when my sister posts a random picture that catches me off guard and I'm glad that at times I still burst into heavy, painful sobs, because it shows they meant something. They mattered to me. And I loved them.

But for my dad, right now, today........there's nothing. Nothing to miss. He was never alive to me anyway. How sad. How shit. But it is what it is.

17/11/18

People know I'm writing a book about all this now, and someone asked me the other day how it will end. I said, I haven't a bloody clue to be honest. How do you end a book about grief? Grief has no end.

My mind this week has been mulling it over – loads. I keep having an image in my head of getting a box and finding all the little bits that mean something about my dad together in one place and putting them together in this box. I have in my mind that New Year's Eve would be a good time to do it. My plan is that I neatly wrap this up and put it away. I don't really feel that it serves me to keep looking at it right now. It feels like old news. How sad is that? It's now just short of nine weeks since he died, and I feel as though I'm done with it, ready to put it away, ready to release any power that It might have once had. Maybe that's squashing my emotions.... maybe it's denial of the pain underneath.... maybe I have actually done all I needed to do. Everyone will have a different opinion I suppose. But I really do feel done with it. I just feel like I need to gather up any little loose ends, any photos, any letters, anything that relates to him and get it all neatly boxed away. I could burn it, I could rip everything up, I could just whack what little bits and bobs I have in the bin, but I don't feel like that's what I need to do. I feel like to do that would be sort of trying to erase this from existence and I don't actually want to do that. I feel as though for the first time ever I really own my story about my dad. It's not full of mystery, hope and confusing reactions. I feel like my story is clear in my head – he left, he didn't bother – he died – the end. And somehow, today, that kind of feels ok. Not completely ok because its shit, and it will always be shit. But it feels complete, and it feels solid and I feel as though I know how to carry it now. And I need to carry it in a box. It needs to be there to revisit if ever I need to. It needs to be there to show others. Maybe my children one day will ask me to tell this story, who knows. It just needs to be there, because it's my story. My life. My dad.

And, for whatever reason, for me, it needs to be in a box.

I'm trusting my inner voice and trusting that this is the direction I need to take to heal.

I suppose I'd better go and buy a box then.

24/11/18

It seems to be on my mind all the time that my dad is dead, but at the moment there's no emotion with that. It feels really weird. Kind of surreal. Sometimes I wonder, "did it actually happen?" and "is he really dead?". It's almost like I'm so used to him being gone, because he's always been gone, but I can't quite accept the fact that he's actually gone now forever. I'm sort of expecting him to turn up but at the same time I know he's not going to. It's just that thing again where your heart and head don't meet.

It's just all so weird. So empty but so consuming at the same time. But I feel like time passing and life going back to 'normal' has stopped the emotions, and I miss them. I miss the raging anger, the tears, the sadness. I miss all that, because then in a weird kind of way I was involved in my dad's life. Now, there's nothing. It's back to nothing. The world has moved on. The funeral is done, and it's just back to nothing. I'm just a woman in her 30's whose dad is dead — that's not all that uncommon. But I feel so different. So out of place, so weird. I sort of want to keep talking about it to people. I want to voice how I feel but at the same time I don't really know how I feel. But I know people don't really need me rambling on at them, and actually I don't really want to be rambling on and dwelling over it all the time either, I just feel like it's been swept under the carpet with and finished too soon. I'm not ready to put this experience down and just move on yet. It's almost like I want to drag it out in a way. I want to keep hold of it. Probably because it's the very last experience of my dad I'll ever have. There won't be any more stories to tell about him. No more memories, no more awkward, uncomfortable meetings, with the ever-present glimmer of hope that he'll magically become the dad I always longed for. Nope, none of that is ever happening. All I've got is this — his death. This is the last piece. The final chapter. And I don't want to put it down because it's finished then forever, and he's well and truly gone, and I just don't want that. I never wanted that. I never wanted my dad to be gone, but he is. Permanently this time, without question, without hope, he's gone. And that is shit. It feels shit. Its bizarre feeling so empty, but at the same time so full. Full of questions, full of unfinished business, full of emotions, but nowhere for them to go. It's like it's just there, in the pit of my stomach, held there like a big lump, and I don't really know what to do with it, because actually, as uncomfortable as it feels, I kind of want to keep hold of it for now. I'm not ready to let it go. I'm not ready to let him go.

08/12/18

Yesterday a colleague was talking about her ex-husband and how horrible he was being to their children. She was worried that her kids would be damaged because they had such an awful father. He was rejecting them continuously and now they were getting older and realising that their dad is in fact, a massive prick. She was sad about it, she felt guilty about it. My heart broke for her. I said to her, "that man you had children with, didn't turn up to your first date being a massive nobhead did he?" She said no. I told her, "he didn't come with a massive sign around his neck saying, 'I'm a complete arsehole and in a few years' time, after we've had children, I'm going to show you just what a nasty bastard I am'. If he had, I imagine you wouldn't have bothered with a second date." She said no, she would have run a mile.

Sometimes I get angry with my mam, I think 'for fuck sake could you not have chosen someone better to be my dad?' But she was just like this lady, she didn't see it coming either. I didn't make the best choice of father for my children either, and sometimes I feel guilty for that. It's only natural. We want the best for our children, we want the best fathers for our children, but it's out of our hands really. You can't make someone be a good dad, you can't change people. It's hard enough to change ourselves.

I've learned that bitterness gets you nowhere. Anger is understandable, but it ultimately gets you nowhere. If I sit here and get angry at my dad, angry at my mam, angry at my ex, or anyone in fact, then I'm just drinking poison and expecting it to kill the people I'm angry with. It won't work. It doesn't work. It will only ever kill me. When anger comes to visit me, I acknowledge it, I say 'I see you anger, I know why you're here' but then I spit it out. I 'exorcise' it from me. You need to get it out of your body in whatever safe way you can, because if you keep it in and allow it to stay there and fester, it will destroy you from the inside.

The only thing we have complete power and control over is ourselves. So, concentrate on being the best version of you that you can be.

Yes, children of dickhead dads have some 'issues', have some pain, of course we do, we got rejected by a parent for fucks sake, that's not a pleasant experience. But I'm still here, I'm still a good person, I'm still standing, it hasn't destroyed me, and it won't destroy your children either.

My advice to that colleague was to just show the children what good parenting looks like; what natural healthy emotions look like, show them that you love them. Allow them to be upset, and tell them that's OK. Just be there when they need you. That's all you can do, that's all anyone can do. The children will decide in their own time what their feelings are towards their dad, and children aren't daft usually. They tend to spot where they aren't loved and gravitate back to where they are.

Being dumped by your dad is shit. Being dumped by my dad was seriously shit, but it's my story, it's my life, I've made peace with it. There's always going to be a part of me that thinks, 'It would've been really nice to have had a good dad; to know what that felt like to experience being a daddy's girl.' But I won't. And I can dwell on it for the rest of my life or I can accept it as my story and make the best of what I have got. And for me, the absence of my dad meant that I had three parents growing up — my mam, my gran and my granda — and I wouldn't actually ever change that. If I had the magic time machine that would make life so much easier and I could go back to being eight and I could change my dad and make him stay, I actually wouldn't. I really wouldn't. I love that I saw so much of my grandparents, I love that my heart breaks so painfully when I think about them, because it means I had something special. Something so unbelievably special. I'm glad I miss them so much, I'm glad that it hurts so much, because it means they meant something to me, it means I loved them, and actually if my dad had been around, I wouldn't have had all that time with them.

So, I genuinely wouldn't change it.

My dad leaving also made room for my step dad, and as bonkers as he is, I can't imagine our family without him in it. I don't want my family to not have him in it.

If I did have the magic time machine, what I would actually do is go back to my eight-year-old self and tell her this,

"Wendz, I need to tell you something about your dad. Your dad is ill, his brain is broken, and his heart is broken, and he doesn't know how to be a dad. His heart won't let him love people properly and his brain isn't working well enough for him to realise that there's something wrong. He's really poorly, but he won't take any medicine for it right now either, so he's gone away to try and get better. It could take years and years, and no one knows right now if he'll ever get better.

You need to know that him being ill is not your fault, it's not your mam's fault, and this kind of illness he has is very very rare. No one else in your family has it, and they won't get it either. You don't have this illness and you won't get it.

Your mam and your grandparents love you so much, and trust me, they are enough to keep you safe, teach you everything you ever need to know and will always be there for you. You're going to have some fantastic times with them so let yourself enjoy it.

I know sometimes you're going to get upset that your dad isn't here and that's ok, that's natural, so you cry when you need to. It's natural to get angry, but try not to get too angry, and don't get upset with your mam, or your sisters, or your grandparents because they haven't done anything wrong.

You need to know that you are such a wonderful little girl; you're funny, you make people laugh, you're clever, you love to be outside, you love to play, so just keep doing all that. Keep being you, don't change a thing about you because you are perfect just as you are."

And I would cuddle her. I'd squeeze that little child so tight and tell her to cry, tell her to cry and cry and cry, but not to change, not to think any of it is her fault, not to be angry. I would just allow her to cry for as long she wanted.

Because no one back then let me cry. My sister told me not to on the night my mam told us he wouldn't be living with us anymore. So, I learned to cry without making a sound. But what I really wanted was to be allowed to sob, and howl and to be hugged and squeezed and told it would be OK.

I genuinely wouldn't bring my dad back into my life with the magic time machine. But I would bring in permission right from day one to feel shit about him leaving.

So, squeeze those kids if you're reading this as a parent with children who have been dumped by their dads. Squeeze them, let them cry, let them howl, and tell them the problem is with their dad, not them. Us kids were always enough, always good enough, our dads were the ones that were broken, and that was never our fault.

24/12/18

I'd imagined that I was going to finish this book on New Year's Eve. I was going to have a little 'ceremony' of sorts, to put all the little pieces I have relating to my dad; the odd photo, letter, there really isn't much, into one box and put it away somewhere nicely.

It doesn't somehow feel as necessary to do now.

I feel like mentally I'm done with it.

It kind of feels like a relief this Christmas to be honest. I don't have to wonder if I'll actually get a card, I know I won't. I don't need to worry about him turning up unexpectedly or causing any dramas, I know he won't. It feels better, lighter, easier. There's no feeling rejected, left out, hurt, etc etc because he's dead. He's gone. It's finished as much as it can ever be.

My Christmas gift to myself has been to finish this book. To put the pieces of my broken relationship with my dad neatly away in my brain and heart. I'm ready to leave it alone now. I feel ok with how things are. It'll never be OK that he did what he did; it was shit and I deserved better. But I'm ok to leave it alone now and just move forward with my life.

My greatest wish for whoever reads my book is that they'll be able to do the same, because it feels so much better to release it.

THE END OF SOMETHING NEVER ENDING

As soon as I realised that my diary scribbles and notes on my phone were becoming a book I wondered, how the hell would I end it? How do you end a book about something like this? Grief and loss – its very nature means it doesn't have an end.

Well, I guess for me it ends something like this……

I choose to feel sorry for him, to pity him, to feel sad for him. Doing that allows a space for love and compassion to come into that void where a loving, nurturing relationship should have been.

I could choose anger, hurt and bitterness. But that's not for me – not anymore. That's not what I choose for myself.

So, going forward I choose to have feelings of love. Love towards myself and my own inner child that deserved so much better. And strangely, love towards my dad too. Does he deserve it? Probably not. But forgiveness in my opinion isn't about soothing the other person. It isn't about giving my dad something nice that he doesn't deserve. The forgiveness is for *my* benefit, it's to sooth and heal *me*. To make me feel better, to make my life more peaceful, to fill my whole being with peace, love and healing instead of bitterness and hate.,

You do whatever you need to do to heal you. I certainly won't judge you for whatever it is you need to do. I know you will do what's right for you, and that is always the way with grief – follow your own inner voice, follow your heart.

I feel as though writing this book, having it all fall out in a messy, ranty, wordy kind of vomit has been the medicine I needed. It's purged it from me and has allowed me the luxury of going over and over it, until it made sense to me.

A part of my mind, heart and soul that had previously been a total bomb site of pain and destruction has now been cleared, tidied, sorted out and now feels so much better. And I feel like this book, this wordy, ranty, emotional vomit might just be a little shoot of goodness that's found a way to grow underneath the years of devastation. Kind of like the film Wall-E when the world has been filled with so much rubbish that it needed to be evacuated, but a tiny plant still manages to grow.

(If you've never seen wall-E I highly recommend you give it a go – it's very profound for a kids' film and just ridiculously cute)

So, here I am, at the end of my journey – sort of. It's the end of the books journey anyway.

This story of mine, just like your story with your dad, will always go everywhere with you. You can't leave it with someone else to look after, and you can't just wipe it from existence. It's there – always – because it's part of you. It's like your shadow, sometimes you can't see it or don't notice it but it's there, it's always there.

So, I urge you to find peace with that part of you. Don't run from it, don't pretend it doesn't exist. Because you can't outrun your own shadow, you can't outrun your own story, it's only going to run as fast as you.

Face it.

Turn, and face it.

Look it in the eyes, knowing that you're stronger than it, and face it.

Then make peace with it.

Make peace with it so you can carry it peacefully, quietly, and on your own terms for the remainder of your days.

That, above all, is my greatest wish for you. You amazing, strong, powerhouses of women who are reading this book. You grew up knowing all too well the pain of being ditched and feeling rejected, but you carried on.

You beautiful, wonderful, fantastic little girls who cried for the loss of your dads, you deserved better!

You were, and still are, worth better!

You should've had better than that!

My wish to you is that you know, and let it sink in to the very core of your soul that you were always enough! It was never your fault, and you deserved better!

I hope you can let that sink in. I hope you can say it over and over again until it sinks in. I hope you can believe the absolute, whole hearted, honest truth of it.

Within you is the strength to carry this experience forever. It's yours. It belongs to you. Your story with your dad, however that looks, is unique to you. And now that he's gone, you write the ending. His story ends with 'He Died'. Your story says… 'Her dad died, so she…' And the rest is up to you.

Mine went a bit like this…

'Her dickhead dad died so she had a right old fucking emotional nightmare for a few months. Then she wrote a book that helped her heal and make peace

with her story of her dad. She let go of all the shite thoughts about herself caused by being a kid whose dad was crap and didn't love her like he should've.

She rested for a bit.

Then she rose!

Without that old shite dragging her down she flew. And she felt fucking fantastic!'

Write the next chapter of your story!

Tell me how it goes for you. I'll be over the moon if it says something like, "And she rose, like the mother fucking queen she was born to be!'

Let that be your next chapter.

Let that be the happily ever after of your own, slightly fucked up in the middle through no fault of your own, fairy tale.

From one ditched daughter to another, you can totally do this! You hold the keys to your own healing, and *you* can release your grief.

ABOUT THE AUTHOR

Somehow, I can manage to write a whole book about myself, and then cringe completely at the prospect of completing this section! Weird I know. So, you already know a lot from reading this but what you might not know is that as well as being employed as a counsellor I also run my own business called Soul Page Holistics.

I have a bit of a 'woo-woo' side. I'm very much into crystals, angels, spirituality, dreams, and basically all things weird and wonderful. I find it fascinating! So much so that I founded an amazing Facebook group called the Soul Searchers Movement where we chat about all this stuff. My favourite place to be is the beach. I have a very needy and affectionate border collie called Winston who often comes with me to 'splodge' in the sea. I spend way too much of my life on social media and even though I can write ridiculously quickly it takes me forever to read books and I rarely finish any.

So, there we have it, phew, I'm glad this section is over.

CONNECT WITH THE AUTHOR

You can follow my blog;

The-Art-Of-Evolving.com

My business page on Facebook is;

https://www.facebook.com/soulpageholistics/

You are very welcome to join The Soul Searchers Movement here;

https://www.facebook.com/groups/406157026812682/

You are also very welcome to email me at soulpageholistics@gmail.com

I look forward to hearing from you and if you have enjoyed this book, I would be extremely grateful if you could leave a review on Amazon.

Thank you

Printed in Great Britain
by Amazon

37514586R00046